Plants Fight Back

DISCOVER THE CLEVER ADAPTATIONS PLANTS USE TO SURVIVE!

WORDS BY
LISA J. AMSTUTZ
PICTURES BY
REBECCA EVANS

To Rebekah, with love

—LJA

For Lainey and Declan, because you're never too old to
get excited about seeing your name in a book!

—RE

Internal Images © Dan Minkin/Creative commons 4.0, Jarek Tuszyński/Creative commons 3.0, John Tann/Creative commons 2.0, Amada44/
Creative commons 3.0, Rameshng/Creative commons 3.0, Whistling Thorn/ Creative commons 2.0, Kbh3rd/Creative commons 3.0,
Katja Schulz/Creative commons 2.0, Elf/Creative commons 3.0, Mokkie/Creative commons 3.0, Jason Hollinger/Creative commons 2.0,
JoeGough/Getty Images, Ardely/Getty Images

Published by Dawn Publications, an imprint of Sourcebooks eXplore
P.O. Box 4410, Naperville, Illinois 60567–4410
(630) 961-3900
sourcebookskids.com

Library of Congress Cataloging-in-Publication Data is on file with the publisher.

Source of Production: Wing King Tong Paper Products Co. Ltd., Shenzhen, Guangdong Province, China
Date of Production: May 2022
Run Number: 5026401

Printed and bound in China.
WKT 10 9 8 7 6 5 4 3

It's tough being rooted
when danger is near.
So what do plants do?
Do they tremble in fear?
Do they give up the fight?
Wait for help to appear?

NO!

Whenever plants find themselves
under attack,
they use their defenses.
That's right...

Plants fight back!

Some species bristle
with needles so prickly,
a grazer who grabs one
will spit it out quickly!

Cactus plants come in all shapes and sizes. Their sharp spines
protect them from being eaten by most desert animals.

Some hire guards
to keep browsers away;
they pay them with housing
and three meals a day.

Biting ants "guard" whistling thorn acacia trees by keeping hungry giraffes from eating the leaves. In return, the tree makes special food for the ants, and its hollow thorns give the ants a safe place to live.

Some fold their leaves and pretend to be dead,
in hopes that a predator might be misled.

A mimosa plant quickly folds its leaves together when it's touched.
The moving leaves scare away insects. Tapirs and other animals
avoid the closed-up leaves because they look like dead twigs.

Some plants deliver a peppery punch to mammals who might try to munch them for lunch.

Rabbits like to eat most garden plants. But they don't touch chili peppers! That's because chili seeds taste very hot to mammals. The hot seeds don't bother birds.

Some warn their neighbors
when danger is near.
That way they can get
their defenses in gear.

When tent caterpillars attack a willow, the tree sends out warning signals through its roots. Nearby willows receive the message. Then they chemically change their leaves to make them taste bad.

Biting these leaves
can cause serious pain.
A tabby who tastes them
won't do it again.

People grow dieffenbachia as a houseplant for its beautiful leaves. But it's poisonous! A pet that bites into a leaf will end up with a painful, swollen mouth and tongue.

Some slip on armor—
a fine gritty suit.
No sensible snacker
wants sand in his snoot!

Sand verbena traps blowing sand on its sticky stems and leaves. The sand covers the plant in a protective coating, like armor. Animals don't like to eat sand!

Others make oodles of
thick, sticky glue.
Intruders soon find themselves
trapped in the goo.

Sticky geranium **oozes** a natural glue from its stem and
leaves. Insects get stuck and can't escape. Then
predators, like this spider, can easily pick them off.

Some are so toxic,
their poison can kill.
Even their touch can
make animals ill.

Fig Tree
☑ OKAY TO EAT 🍈🍉

Manchineel trees grow among other tropical trees, like this fig and trumpet tree. Animals know to stay away from the deadly manchineel. Its fruit is poisonous, and its sap causes blisters.

Touching some leaflets can cause one to itch.
It's really important to know which is which!

Some plants can sting like a wasp or an ant.
It's painful to brush against that sort of plant.

Even a slight touch of poison ivy or nettle leaves can create a burning, painful rash. It's caused by the oil on poison ivy and by the needle-like hairs that cover nettles.

Some wear disguises to hide in plain sight,
in hopes hungry herbivores won't take a bite.

Stone plants blend in with the rocks on the desert floor. Zebras and other grazing animals don't notice them, so the plants don't get eaten.

And sometimes, when plants find life's getting too rough,
they call in the air force. Enough is enough!

When cotton plants are being eaten by
caterpillars, they send out an "SOS signal"—
an invisible cloud of chemicals—into the air.
Wasps get the signal and fly in to get rid of
the caterpillars.

Eating your veggies is healthy, it's true.
And the ones in your lunchbox
are all safe to chew.

But a grazer in search
of a tasty green snack
had better look twice...
'cause that plant
might fight back!

It's Not Easy Being Green

Plants are part of every food chain. That means lots of animals want to eat them! Plants don't have teeth, horns, or claws. They can't even run away! But they "fight back" with clever adaptations that help them survive.

Some Plants Act Tough

Bighorn sheep are one of the few desert animals that can eat **cacti**. They use their horns and hooves to carefully remove the spines.

The sandy coating that covers **sand verbena** wears down the teeth of animals that try to eat it. Flowers are yellow or bright pink.

The hairs on **nettles** act like needles. When touched, they inject a toxin into the skin.

Some Plants Play Tricks

Stone plants can go for months without water. When grown as houseplants, they can live up to fifty years.

Mimosa leaflets respond to touch by releasing water at their base, which causes them to fold up. The leaves reopen after several minutes.

A **sticky geranium** is covered in gooey hairs that trap small insects. The plant then dissolves the insects' bodies and absorbs the nutrients.

Some Plants Find Helpers

Four different kinds of stinging ants compete to live inside the hollow thorns of **whistling thorn acacia**. The ants make holes in the thorns, and when the wind blows through it makes a whistling sound.

Birds help **chili peppers** spread their seeds by eating the fruit and passing the seeds in their droppings.

Wasps can detect the chemicals released by **cotton plants** from a mile away. They fly in and lay their eggs inside the attacking caterpillars. When the wasp larvae hatch, they eat the caterpillars from the inside out.

Some Plants Use Chemicals

Both **poison ivy** and **poison oak** have three leaves that cause a rash. Remember: Leaves of three, let them be.

Imagine how painful it would be to chew a piece of glass. That's how people describe the pain of biting into a **dieffenbachia** leaf.

The fruit of the **manchineel** is called "death apple." Signs are posted to warn people that this tree is poisonous.

Literacy Connection

Tips for Reading Aloud

1. Begin by reading the title and the name of the author and illustrator. Ask and discuss by creating a list on the board. *Can plants fight? Who do they fight? How do they fight?*

2. Read aloud the rhyming verses and show the illustrations. Stop to clarify words if needed (refer to the glossary). But don't read the bonus facts until the second reading.

3. Read the book a second time, both the verses and the additional information. Add to the list on the board.

3. Ask the opening questions from tip one again, writing students' responses on the board under headings "How Plants Fight" and "Who Plants Fight." Clarify that plants don't "fight" the way we usually think of fighting, such as hitting, biting, or kicking. But plants have developed adaptations to protect themselves from being eaten.

5. When you read the final page, ask students the following questions: *Who is the "grazer" in the illustration?* A fawn. *What are the raccoons doing?* Trying to get the children's food. Be sure to explain to students that raccoons might look cute, but they can be dangerous. People should never feed a raccoon or get too close.

6. Read "I've Got an Idea!" and discuss the personal experience that illustrator Rebecca Evans had with a manchineel tree in Costa Rica. Look in the illustration for the animals she actually saw.

7. Read aloud and discuss the information in "Explore More for Kids."

8. Conclude by doing the STEAM Challenge and celebrate with a Plant Party Salad.

Glossary

1. **browser:** an animal that feeds on high-growing, woody plants

2. **bristle:** to be covered with

3. **grazer:** an animal that feeds on grass or other low-growing plants

4. **herbivore:** an animal that eats plants

5. **larva:** the juvenile stage of certain insects; sometimes called caterpillars

6. **poisonous:** able to cause death or illness; toxic

7. **predator:** an animal that eats other organisms

8. **snoot:** nose or snout

9. **spine:** a type of leaf that forms a sharp point

10. **toxic:** able to cause death or illness; poisonous

I've Got an Idea!

Where do authors and illustrations get their ideas? Here's what inspired author Lisa Amstutz and illustrator Rebecca Evans.

Lisa: My thesis research focused on plant/insect interactions. I've always been fascinated by the ways plants move, adapt, communicate, and protect themselves. I'd been thinking about writing a book on plant defenses, and one day the first stanza popped into my head. I jotted it down and went from there!

Rebecca: While visiting Costa Rica, I took photos of a manchineel tree growing on the beach. They became the references for this book. As my illustration shows, the manchineel had a warning sign in front of it, and lots of amazing animals in nearby trees—a sloth, capuchin monkeys, howler monkeys, agoutis, parrots, and toucans.

Science Connection

STEAM Challenge—Plant Defenses

Plants may look like easy targets for herbivores. But in reality, they have a whole arsenal of defense mechanisms ranging from chemicals to camouflage. For this STEAM challenge, students will design a plant with a special adaptation for survival.

STUDY NATURE

Review the structure and function of plant parts. Refer to "Plant Party." Ask students to identify and describe the unique and interesting structures and functions of the plants in the book. Research other plants through actual observation, in books, or via the internet.

SOLVE A PROBLEM

Plants have a problem. They're part of every food chain and are eaten by a wide variety of mammals, birds, and insects. They've solved this problem with clever adaptations. Refer to the categories on "Explore More for Kids."

DESIGN A PLANT

Have students design a plant that includes all six plant parts. Ask them to identify an animal that would eat the plant and then determine which plant part (or parts) will "fight back."

CREATE A MODEL

Engineers build models. So do many artists! Provide a variety of craft supplies for students to use to make a model of their plant. Alternately, have students draw a picture and label it. Ask them to give their plant a catchy or creative name.

PRESENT TO OTHERS

Have students share their picture or model and describe their plant's defense mechanisms. Encourage them to have fun with their explanations by "nominating" their plant to become an MVP (Most Valuable Plant) or to be inducted into the Plant Hall of Fame.

Let's Have a Plant Party

Roots, stems, leaves, flowers, fruit, and seeds are the parts of plants. Each part helps plants grow and reproduce. Using the labeled diagram of a chili pepper, identify each plant part (structure) and discuss what the part does (function).

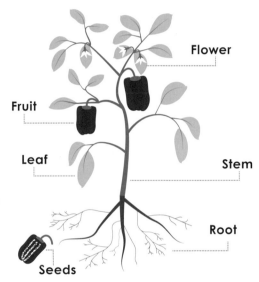

Roots hold the plant in the soil and soak up water and nutrients for the plant to use

Stems carry water and nutrients from the roots to the leaves

Leaves take in air and sunlight to make food. This process is called photosynthesis (meaning "made with light").

Flowers—After pollination, a part of a flower becomes a fruit

Fruits contain seeds

Seeds grow into new plants

Return to the illustrations in the book and have students identity the part of each plant that "fights back." Some parts might be hard to identify. For example, a cactus spine is actually a modified leaf, and a thorn is a modified stem.

Celebrate with a "Plant Party" by making a salad that includes all six plant parts. Here are some suggestions: ROOTS (carrots, radishes, green onions, beets); STEMS (celery, asparagus); LEAVES (lettuce, spinach, chard); FLOWERS (broccoli, cauliflower); FRUITS (tomatoes, beans, cucumbers, apples); and SEEDS (sunflower seeds, pumpkin seeds, peas, corn).

A Few More Recommendations from Dawn Publications

Nature Did It First: Engineering Through Biomimicry—Got a problem? More than likely nature has solved it! Look outside and you will see a world full of amazing engineering designs. Part playful poetry, part fascinating nonfiction.

Silent Swoop: An Owl, an Egg, and a Warm Shirt Pocket—An owl swoops down to lay her egg in a coal yard—a dangerous spot for a fragile egg. Miraculously, the egg hatches! A tender story of rescue, rehabilitation, and most of all friendship.

What's in the Garden?—Good food doesn't begin on a store shelf with a box. It comes from a garden bursting with life! Gorgeously detailed and realistic illustrations.

Earth Heroes: Champions of Wild Animals—A collection of biographies of men and women who helped save ten key species of animals, from eagles to elephants. For upper elementary and middle school.

If You Love Honey: Nature's Connections—Honey links together dandelions, earthworms, mushrooms, an old oak tree, and even blue jays squawking in its branches. If you love honey, you're connected to all of nature.

Also Illustrated by Rebecca Evans

Why Should I Walk? I Can Fly!—A little bird, a big sky, and the first time out of the nest! A robin's first flight is a gentle reminder about what we can accomplish if we just keep trying.

If You Played Hide-and-Seek with a Chameleon—What would happen if you played games with animals? Sports, science, and math come together in twelve outrageous competitions. Win or lose, it's hilarious fun!

If Animals Built Your House—You could lick gobs of honey off your walls if you lived in a beehive. Or maybe you'd prefer snuggling into a leafy chimp nest high in the rain forest canopy. Twelve amazing animal architects just might have the perfect house for you!

 Dawn Publications is dedicated to inspiring in children a deeper understanding and appreciation for all life on Earth.

 **Lisa Amstutz** discovered that writing was a way to combine her love of books with her love of nature. Drawing on her background in biology and environmental science, she specializes in topics related to science and agriculture. Although this is Lisa's first book for Dawn Publications, she has written over one hundred children's books! When she's not writing, you might find her birding, scrapbooking, or enjoying a cup of tea and a good book. Lisa lives with her family on a small-scale farm in Ohio. Visit her at lisaamstutz.com.

 **Rebecca Evans** started drawing as soon as she could hold a crayon and just never stopped. After working for nine years as an artist and designer, she returned to her first love—children's book illustration. She's authored and/or illustrated twenty books; this is her fourth book for Dawn. Rebecca is also a Regional Co-Advisor for her SCBWI chapter. She lives in Maryland and enjoys spending time with her husband and four young children, while working from her home studio during every spare moment. Find her at rebeccaevans.net.